Trespassing on the Mount of Olives

The Poiema Poetry Series

Poems are windows into worlds; windows into beauty, goodness, and truth; windows into understandings that won't twist themselves into tidy dogmatic statements; windows into experiences. We can do more than merely peer into such windows; with a little effort we can fling open the casements, and leap over the sills into the heart of these worlds. We are also led into familiar places of hurt, confusion, and disappointment, but we arrive in the poet's company. Poetry is a partnership between poet and reader, seeking together to gain something of value—to get at something important.

Ephesians 2:10 says, "We are God's workmanship..." *poiema* in Greek—the thing that has been made, the masterpiece, the poem. The Poiema Poetry Series presents the work of gifted poets who take Christian faith seriously, and demonstrate in whose image we have been made through their creativity and craftsmanship.

These poets are recent participants in the ancient tradition of David, Asaph, Isaiah, and John the Revelator. The thread can be followed through the centuries—through the diverse poetic visions of Dante, Bernard of Clairvaux, Donne, Herbert, Milton, Hopkins, Eliot, R. S. Thomas, and Denise Levertov—down to the poet whose work is in your hand. With the selection of this volume you are entering this enduring tradition, and as a reader contributing to it.

—D.S. Martin
Series Editor

Trespassing on the Mount of Olives

Poems in Conversation with the Gospels

BRAD DAVIS

CASCADE *Books* • Eugene, Oregon

TRESPASSING ON THE MOUNT OF OLIVES
Poems in Conversation with the Gospels

The Poiema Poetry Series

Copyright © 2021 Brad Davis. All rights reserved. Except for brief quotations in critical publications or reviews, no part of this book may be reproduced in any manner without prior written permission from the publisher. Write: Permissions, Wipf and Stock Publishers, 199 W. 8th Ave., Suite 3, Eugene, OR 97401.

Cascade Books
An Imprint of Wipf and Stock Publishers
199 W. 8th Ave., Suite 3
Eugene, OR 97401

www.wipfandstock.com

PAPERBACK ISBN: 978-1-6667-3082-1
HARDCOVER ISBN: 978-1-6667-2279-6
EBOOK ISBN: 978-1-6667-2280-2

Cataloguing-in-Publication data:

Names: Davis, Brad.
Title: Trespassing on the mount of olives : poems in conversation with the gospels / Brad Davis.
Description: Eugene, OR: Cascade Books, 2021 | The Poiema Poetry Series
Identifiers: ISBN 978-1-6667-3082-1 (paperback) | ISBN 978-1-6667-2279-6 (hardcover) | ISBN 978-1-6667-2280-2 (ebook)
Subjects: LCSH: subject | subject | subject | subject
Classification: CALL NUMBER 2021 (paperback) | CALL NUMBER (ebook)

09/08/21

The cover image, "Olive Tree with Broken Branch" by Barry Moser, is used with permission of the artist.

for my students
(1987–2019)

*When they had sung a hymn, they went out
to the Mount of Olives.*
>   MATTHEW 26:30, MARK 14:26

*A fragment of earth seen through leaves,
through the thicket of time, at last through the brook
that covers the bottom of a slender chalice.*
>   KAROL WOJTYLA, FROM HIS POEM "MOUNT OF OLIVES"

"*Forgive us our trespasses.*"
>   JESUS, MATTHEW 6:12

Contents

Preface | ix

Hymn | 1

1

A Mother's Work | 5
Man with Water Jar | 7
Judas of the Suburbs | 10
Crowds | 11
The Women | 12
Patience | 14
That Sabbath | 16
Press Release | 17
At First | 18
My Two Bits | 19
So I Imagine | 20
Bread & Fish | 21
Romsey *Christus* | 23
Federal Regulation Prohibits Resurrection | 25

2

Ἐν ἀρχῇ | 29
This Will Be Misunderstood | 30
Young Elizabeth's Lament | 32
Need | 33
Annunciation | 34
Venit | 35
What Matters Moves | 37
Peace on Earth | 39
A Carol | 40

Midsummer | 41
Ode To The Ferryman | 42
The Magi's Report | 44
The Sword | 45
On Dream Learning | 46

3

Starting from Nazareth | 49
The Watchers | 50
The Manner of Their Leave Taking | 52
Capernaum | 54
Prepping for Bible Study | 55
The Generative Influence of Q on John's Gospel | 56
In John's Gospel | 58
Do Whatever He Tells You | 59
Wilderness | 60
Report from the Field | 61
A Quick Thank You | 63
Do You Want to Get Well? | 64
Before Religion | 65
La La Caveat | 66
The Ear | 67
A Moving Poem | 68
Sometimes | 69
To Separate Head and Body | 70
Confession | 72
Maybe This Is Not a Poem | 73
Parsing | 75
It Would Be Arson | 76
Fraction | 77
The Sign of Jonah | 78
La La Thankful Living | 79
At Table | 80
And When It Is Dry? | 81
Running to Win | 82
Unattended | 83
In Morning Sunlight | 84
Credo | 86

How It Will Be | 87
What Difference Does It Make | 88
They Will Respect My Son | 89
When the End Comes | 90
Do Not Think This Is | 92
When the Sun Stopped Shining | 94

4
Trespassing on the Mount of Olives | 97

Notes | 99
Acknowledgments | 103

Preface

This sequence of poems is a bridge project, like my sequence, *Opening King David: Poems in Conversation with the Psalms* (Wipf & Stock, 2011). *OKD* bridged the three years during which I transitioned from being a boarding school's chaplain to serving the school as an ordinary lay teacher and squash coach.

Beginning in the spring of 2018, it occurred to me a new bridge project might be timely, given that I had just decided that the upcoming school year would be my final year of teaching. To balance the Psalm sequence, a Jesus sequence seemed in order. Over the subsequent three-plus years, I made a slow read of the gospels, letting the birddog process of *lectio divina* flush poems from the convoluted thicket of my psyche. (Many got away, others were mangled, some may still be hunkered down in there; those found here are the few I netted and that seem more or less presentable.) Among the first poems drafted was one that arrived title-first—"Trespassing on the Mount of Olives"—and then suggested itself as the book's title poem. I didn't argue.

The methodology for this project was not as clearly defined as that which I adopted for *OKD*. This time I approached the biblical text more improvisationally. I was not as concerned as I'd been in *OKD* to read a psalm a week and have a poem drafted by that Saturday. Nor was I concerned to draft one poem per chapter or pericope. I set out simply to sit with the text and listen for and to the Word. "In the beginning was the Word, and the Word was with God, and the Word was God . . . , and the Word became flesh and pitched his tent among us." (John 1:1 and 1:14)

We live in a day when it is important to allow persons to identify themselves from what they know of themselves and not to impose identities on them based on however we may see them. I chose to approach the Jesus of the gospels in this way. (I took greater liberties with secondary characters.) While it is impossible to escape entirely one's biases, I tried to let the gospels' singular portrait of Jesus inform my answer to the question he put to his friends: "Who do you say I am?" (Luke 9:20) A wonderfully

Preface

complex portrait, and I brought a tangled complex of resistance and limitation to the process of attending to it. One little phrase found in the synoptic gospels served to keep me on task; when Jesus is transfigured in front of three of his closest friends, a voice speaks from an enveloping cloud and says to the friends, "This is my son, whom I love. *Listen to him.*" (Mark 9:6) Which was my primary aim. The poems followed.

Finally, what should be obvious: these are poems, not doctrinal or evangelistic treatises. Their task, by the mercy of God, is to work and wear well as poems.

grace&peace

HYMN Matthew 26:30
Mark 14:26

In praise of *That
than which
nothing greater
can be conceived*,

what when once
named—the name
a placeholder—acquires
conceivability and so

cannot be That.
Though who doesn't love
a metaphor;
the vehicle, not

counting equality with
the tenor a thing
to be grasped,
contents itself with

serving to draw
attention to, bring out
the natural colors of
the served, finally happy

to concede the deferential
gap between
contingent this and
uncanny That. So: *hen*,

*father, still small voice, light,
lamb,* and on and on . . .

1

A MOTHER'S WORK   *Luke 21:37–38*

We sleep in a grove
outside the city
on the Mount of Olives.
Though I rise early,
he has already
left for the temple.
Every day for weeks now,
the people wait for him.
Temple leaders, too,
except to trap him.
He does not see this
ending well, but we
see the numbers growing.
The crowds love him.

We love him,
and we are waiting—
our patience
sorely tested—for him
to spark the fire
he said he came to
bring upon the earth.
We have seen him
look across the valley
at the city and weep.
We have heard him say
not one stone
will be left on stone,
and then the new will come.

Each morning on this hill
it is my job
to rouse the others.
He will need us
to mind the crowd's perimeter,
usher the sick and lame
into his presence
where, by the hand of God,
he makes whole
the host that he, even
greater than Gideon,
will lead to victory,
the fire of God
set upon the earth at last.

MAN WITH WATER JAR *Luke 22:10*

1.
If you look carefully
in the painting's lower left quarter,

just inside the Essene Gate
of the Old City,

you can make out a man
cradling a child-sized water jar.

Milling around him are several women,
their jars balanced

on their shoulders or heads.
The street teems with commerce

and red-caped Roman soldiers
and all manner of priestly comings and goings

to and from the Temple courts.
An ordinary day in the City of Peace,

except there's that man—and two travelers
entering the city who will follow the jar

to a house and a room upstairs in the house
where they will see to it that all is ready.

2.
What does the man cradling
the water jar know of the Teacher?

Given a need for secrecy,
he would not have heard the Teacher

instruct the women to tell the homeowner
to prepare his upper room for *Pesach*.

Likely all the man knows is nothing
more than where to stand and how

to hold the jar and to be watching
for two Galileans who will enter the city

as though looking for someone. Likely
the man is indentured or enslaved—

reliable as the homeowner is
trustworthy—and wants nothing

more than to discharge this duty
and return to his own family by nightfall.

3.
Form fitted to function, class,
and proximity to source;

whether hewn stone or shaped clay,
stitched hide or banded wood—

long before ascending
from the earth of domesticity

to the paradise of metaphor,
the water jar

enabled entire civilizations
their rise and prospering.

So we all are indebted to what-
and whoever delivers us

our daily *dour, ura, ama,*
vatn, tskhali, nero, wai, mmiri,

uisce, thuk, av, aiga, aegoa, amazi,
dlo, d^wr, voda, uisge, water.

4.
But fetching the water
was a servant woman's work;

a manservant's to receive it from her
and distribute as instructed.

Was there shame in being a man
standing with a water jar

near a principal gate
of the holy nation's royal city?

May we assume—and why
not—the manservant suffered

his ordeal for a benefit sufficient
to buoy him through that long afternoon—

something inscrutable
unfolding?

5.
They are the story's unnamed
who move me—the man with water jar,

his wife waiting up for him, each
with faith enough to do the next thing

and hope that perhaps their sparrow-like lives
won't count for nothing—since without

them, their kind, there is no story,
no reason for the story in the first place.

JUDAS OF THE SUBURBS *Matthew 27:3*

Who rises early
to birdsong aiming

to get it all wrong? Even
evildoers feed the cat,

make coffee for visiting in-laws,
sing to themselves

and in the congregation
hymns of a better world—*soon*

and very soon—a balanced
ledger, vindication.

Not every beautiful
brown bird that alights

in the crabapple
can be a waxwing.

CROWDS

Matthew 21:9
Revelation 11:18

Wheeling on thermals,
a duet of osprey high above
West Meadow Beach.
It is April. They are migrating
to a nesting site north
and east of here to repair
with marsh grass and winter kill
their pole-top hatchery.
We few are one crowd,
our attention praise-like—
Blessed are they who come
wheeling in the name of God—
our binoculars kin to the cloaks
once spread before Him.
But there is another crowd,
hunkered in boardrooms
and at three-way lunches,
who labor in the name of
prosperity to reverse
regulations that, decades ago,
made possible the raptors' return.
Do I oversimplify
our choice: with which
crowd will we be numbered?
Those who bless the yellow-eyed,
high-wheeling osprey
or those who destroy the earth.

THE WOMEN *Matthew 27:55*

Safe to say the men were inept
at household management, so the women
had to improvise a micro-economy
fitted to the Teacher's peripatetic style.
Let's say the women not only
kept the men's money purse filled,
they kept one of their own, too.
And let's say the Teacher, finding
the women organized in ways the men
knew nothing of, would commission
the women to do his business—
the men entirely in the dark. So when
subterfuge was required and, say,
a grand, politically freighted entrance
into Jerusalem called for a donkey or two,
the Teacher trusted the women
to make the necessary arrangements.
Or when Passover arrived, the city
on edge, and the Teacher wanted
an upper room prepared for the meal,
all the men knew was, once inside
the city gates, there'd be a man
with a water jar they should follow,
clueless of the women's prior negotiation
with the householder. No doubt
on such forays, the men, finding everything
as the Teacher had instructed them,
assumed it was some kind of miracle, say,
a miracle of foreknowledge.
No wonder, when the end finally came

and the Teacher breathed his last,
the women were there, having been asked
by him to purchase the grave clothes.

PATIENCE   *between Luke 23:56*
                                               and Luke 24:1

We were wrong.
I was wrong
about him.
He was not
supposed to die.
At least not
so soon
or in that way.
O God, remove
the picture
from my mind's eye:

whip-flayed skin,
the blood,
that thorn-bush crown
jammed
down over
his forehead, the full
weight of his body
hung from rope
and nails, that dark sky.
How long, O Lord,
the sight of it?

He told us
to pray for them,
the executioners and those
who arrested him.
But I cannot.
He is so much better
than I. Was

so much better than
any of us. And now what?
I don't know.
I don't know anything any more.

THAT SABBATH *Matthew 27:19–24*

Likely Pilate didn't sleep well.

Likely his dreamy wife refused
    to share the bed with him.

Likely he spent most of the night
    washing and rewashing his hands.

Likely she thought of leaving him.

Likely, come morning, no one thought,
    "What a great day for singing spiritual songs
    or writing a requiem mass or
    what say I paint the Last Supper above that door over there."

Likely theological cartooning had yet
    to commend itself to anyone who had witnessed the execution;
    no one was thinking *new covenant* or *vicarious atonement*
    or *the harrowing of hell* or *the third day*.

Likely no one tried explaining anything to anyone.

Likely no one spoke at all.

PRESS RELEASE   *Mark 16:1–8*

When the old was
wholly itself
and we were
a complete mess,

the new was
conceived in a tomb
when a body was
changed—

which is
our one clear glimpse
of what will be:
all old things completely new.

AT FIRST   *Matthew 28:1*
                                                Mark 16:1

no one believed the women
their fearful stuttering.
Why ever believe nonsense

or women? Yet the grave clothes,
the guard in a panic, that
ridiculous report already out.

Why repeat it now? Think rumor—
mere bunkum—dressed up
for a party the party experts say

has lost its cultural cachet.
But then those women, their
interrupted devotion to a corpse,

that gardener in the cool of the day,
and everything in me wants
to believe them—perhaps already

believes them: Mary Magdalene,
with Salome and Joanna
and Mary the mother of James.

MY TWO BITS *Luke 24:41–42*

You don't know me. No reason you should.
Yet when he asked,
I was the one who served him
the boiled fish I had prepared for the others.
Nothing out of the ordinary.
And when he spooned my fish into his mouth,
I started laughing, something I did
whenever he did the strange, wonderful things he did—
and the men would shush me
and send me on ahead to find a well
or scout out a place for the night.
Sometimes the men were like that with us,
but never the Teacher. He had this way
of speaking to us and including us in the work
that I don't think he mentioned to the men.
So when he received the bowl from my shaking hand,
I knew he was no ghost—and, this time,
no one shushed my laughter,
for we were all laughing and crying at the same time.
Even the Teacher,
who had somehow come back to us.

SO I IMAGINE   *John 20:19–20*

What appears from here impermeable
(you cannot slip an arm through)

is, from the other side, at every point
regardless the avenue of approach,

an open wall, though there are rules
governing those there to honor

the holiness of our being here
and our need of a solitary place

to pray or make love or simply
be undisturbed by any other,

an inner room where one may indeed
be alone and draw near the One

who is never far off, who always
respecting us (improbably) awaits

us there; till one day all will change,
and what appears impermeable

will become for us an open wall,
and we will come and go from here

as we choose, no thought to past
need or preference, for we will be

as he is, who was the first and best of us
from our side to slip full through.

BREAD & FISH   *John 21:4–13*

First breakfast
after the last
supper was a lake

side picnic.
Perhaps he picked
up the bread

in town
or finally worked
his magic

on a few flat stones.
As for the fish,
likely he waded

out a ways
and called one over
to himself, no

words necessary,
he being
the Word, it being

tilapia (from
the Tswana *tlhapi*
meaning

"fish"), perhaps
a mango tilapia—as
long as a dozen

אֶצְבָּעוֹת- and weighing   (etsba-im: fingers)
maybe a full
עֹמֶר.   (omer: 3.5 pounds)

And so
the disciples' catch
of a hundred

fifty-three large
tilapia, even
at two pounds per,

came in
at over three
hundred pounds.

And Peter
dragged the net ashore.
And the net

refused to tear.
And as fascinating
as the details

may be,
it is the singular *who*
that matters—

as is also true
here this morning, west
of Putnam:

namely,
the One there
on the beach,

by the fire and eager
for a breakfast
with friends.

ROMSEY CHRISTUS   John 20:26–29

for sculptor Peter Ball

As a child, I had no name for it,
the man-on-a-cross religion,
our sanctuary like a frightfully
ornate dungeon where priests
played dress-up, performing
ritual acts, vocal and manual—
think necromancers, mediums
calling on the ghost of the twisted
corpse hung above their heads
to change gag-worthy wafers
of pressed, stale bread into flesh,
port wine into blood, and we
ate and drank the ghastly stuff
solemn as mourners at a funeral.

Soon enough I learned we were
Episcopalians, like Catholics
but better dressed. And somehow
our dead Jesus was more alive
than their dead Jesus. Or at least
more handsome, an idealized
British king or Nordic chieftain
who'd been unceremoniously
wrecked by an unwashed horde
of wretched sinners and infidels;
who for us and our salvation
died so we might make gilded
figures of his lifeless body and
fulfill our death cult obligations.

I do apologize to my friends
who reasonably subsist upon
a weekly reenactment of his grisly
execution and re-interment
in their undeserving bodies.
It moves me, too. But I live and
move obsessed, persuaded
his in-breaking—from arrival
in a blest teen's chaste womb
to his final breath and burial—
effected nothing if his body
did not rise, had not been changed
and raised and wondrously
reinstated as reigning over all.

Why ever laud a lifeless form?
Which brings me to your Romsey
Christus, Peter: no cross, only
scars and a wide-eyed, open-arm
gesture of ecstatic welcome;
and look, you have retained
his brown (and glowing) skin,
middle eastern cheeks and nose.
Yes! Him. Alive and desiring
that we take this yoke upon us,
his brown arm across our shoulders,
and learn from him the meaning
of living not into but beyond
death—with all the life he offers.

FEDERAL REGULATION PROHIBITS
RESURRECTION   *Matthew 27:66*

The physical bodies of the once dead are forbidden to undergo translation into spiritual bodies. Every suspicious revivification shall be investigated and, if found to be so changed, prosecuted to the fullest extent of the law.

When asked why the new regulation, a high-ranking federal official replied, "Taxes, taxes, taxes. No physical body, no need of a domicile or job or payment for goods and services. It's just common sense. And supported by the Chamber of Commerce and the Committee on Ways and Means." When pressed, she refused further comment.

But alone in my loft, over mojitos and well off the record, she confessed incredulity that the statute should even exist, given the last recorded resurrection occurred two-thousand plus-or-minus years ago.

"You can never be too safe," I conceded.

"Common sense," she repeated, setting her mojito on the end table and leaning into me.

2

Ἐν ἀρχῇ   John 1:1

the word first then all
worlds to the end
of worlds

and to each
world the word
is light

till each world to be
like the word is
made new

and all things
first to last
are light

THIS WILL BE MISUNDERSTOOD　　　　　*John 1:4–9*

because babel
because where I come from
where you come from
because we are somewhere midway along whatever path this is
to when all will be revealed
and we know fully as we are fully known
do you know the allusion
do you believe in a love that desires
to save the world from itself
do you even think the world needs saving
you and I need saving
from conformity to an unseen pattern
from ourselves
do you believe there could be a better way
because I do
because all my truest heroes did
because if there is not
then why are we wired it seems always
to be inventing always
imagining from earth's beauty
and the excellence of the best among us always
in the direction of art
in the direction of science and seeing
what is out there beyond sight or imagination
and what is in here
in our bodies
our living souls
do you know we will not recognize ourselves when we get there
should we get there
beyond our best ideas of what it means to be human
beyond what anything means

because babel
because hid from our eyes
because we will not get there unless and until *there* comes to us
like light from the sun
like light from the innumerable billions of stars
because love
because ready or not

YOUNG ELIZABETH'S LAMENT   Luke 1:7

Not without much labor have I, like Sarai before me,
resigned myself to being only half a woman.

Yes, I've Zechariah, but will he want to keep me on
when another would provide him a son?

Barren: some say a sign of God's displeasure. So
as for me, *Good morning, worthless one.*

*Greet the glowering sun, unfortunate spouse, quick-judging
neighbors, the never-to-be aunts, uncles, grandparents.*

Is there a more bitter sentence—to be cursed thus
but then denied an exile far removed from

the daily disgrace of coming in and going out?
How to carry on, fetch water—miserably betrayed

by nature—bearing only this: a husband's disappointment.
Behold, O world, the one as-good-as dead.

NEED   *John 1:16*

There is wanting, and loving what is wanted,
a lasting partner, the sweetness of a sparrow's song;

then there is not wanting to want what is wanted,
any obverse universe with loveless benefits—

wanting, not wanting: loving, not loving.
Desire is a sloppy braid pulled too tight at the top

and unsecured at the bottom, coming undone,
utterly confused and confusing altogether.

The Buddha said desire is the problem.
The Christ said desire is tricky and can work

for good, but as there is a problem with desire
that is not desire, the greatest need is grace. Though,

too, there is a problem with even every stab
at understanding—so how about grace upon grace.

ANNUNCIATION *Luke 1:26*

Yesterday, an ordinary girl. This morning, the same birds
singing, same sun bothering me awake, and here,

lying on my same mat, the same chores awaiting me—
yet I do not want to open my eyes.

*

I cannot love my life as I did yesterday,
before . . . whatever it was . . . an unfamiliar

old one . . . who approached slowly and squatted opposite
as I tended the flat bread browning on the coals . . .

who admired my skill and surprised me
by speaking of me strangely and knowing my name.

Then that proposal . . . terrifying . . . though I surprised myself
agreeing to it—no thought to mother's wisdom,

father's assent—and without another word,
the old one rose, bowed, turned,

and left me more alone than I have ever been.

*

I hear my sister stirring on her mat. She will be surprised
I am still beside her and not about my chores.

Can I tell her? And how to explain it to the man I am to wed?
What have I done? Who will listen and understand?

VENIT   *Matthew 1:23*

across distances, arrived
on this improbable sphere
of polarized debris wobbling
on its fortuitous axis and
reverenced by a lifeless moon.
Surely unless he'd known
our planet's whereabouts
he'd not have found the place,
let alone the female here
in whom he would become
the earthling's baby boy.

What is self-evident:
none of this is self-evident.
Some say I should not
think so but only cozy up
to him who made the trip,
become a child of God
and get a job, join a church
and tithe to keep the lights on.
It's not that I do not love
the idea of the Incarnation
or his unlikely resurrection.

I simply cannot buy the line
that we must board a barge
the party calls an ark, or else.
Look, I'm no cosmologist,
merely one who thinks
he sees, stirred by a holy
trove of deep space photos,

what ego or laziness denies:
birds will pick our bones,
and if he is not Immanuel
then nothing matters. Full stop.

WHAT MATTERS MOVES   *Matthew 1:20*

An angel in the dream inside Joseph's head.
Janeway in Leonardo's studio inside Holodeck 3.
But whereas the captain has no being outside the show,
the angel lives independently of Matthew's narrative,
like but not like the one in my dream with whom
I share a walkup loft studio in a pre-war fabric mill
refitted for micro-businesses and hipsters like us.
If he has a name, he's not telling. Says it's not important.
I suspect if he ever let on, the mill would collapse
or burst into flame. So who needs to know? What matters
moves beyond the property of words. He comes
and goes. Sleeps in the northwest corner. In the dream,
when I arrive he's already out cold. I never thought
angels needed sleep, but maybe his is a harder labor
than I think. Maybe navigating the heaviness
of our humid nights wears on him as he insinuates
himself into whatever within a brain ignites as dream.
Which, come to think of it, would make for a cool
video game: The good guy, an angel of the LORD, sent
to deliver one little word—at every level, a perfect word—
to a sleeping hero bereft of wisdom for the peril at hand.
(God gives to his beloved sleep.) And each player,
hugging a joystick and killer weapons array, fights
through scores of seductions, onslaughts, brilliantly
conceived deceptions, any number of vivid dreams other
than the one intended as the game's true destination.
And having cleared the angel's path to the ultimate level,
costuming becomes the issue, as all have their own
notions of what an angel looks like. For how else
will a sleeping hero recognize instantly a winded,

battle-weary dream-being as the Lord's ambassador?
O, the choices, the innumerable pitfalls, the call
for moves well beyond the property of words.

PEACE ON EARTH   *Luke 2:8–20*

As a child I thought if only my story had angels in it, then they'd listen, take my little life seriously. So when I'd go into town after tending my lambs, people wouldn't hold their noses. They'd ask me to tell again the story about the angels.

Decades later, it happened. Two of us had night duty. The campfire shone brightly. It was my watch, and the wolves, their eyes like fierce red stars on the horizon, kept their distance from the sheep. Out of nowhere, an eerie glow appeared above our campsite. It became brighter than the fire, though I didn't need to squint to look at it. I called out to my partner and grabbed my staff. Awake, armed, and terrified, we watched something that looked like a man step down toward us, stop, and speak to us with such respect as we would speak to a prince.

As he finished, the light engulfed us, and we forgot about the wolves. And there were hundreds more like him, all singing a song over and over. We tried singing it too, but, as suddenly as the angels had arrived, they disappeared. It wasn't until we settled down that we were able to piece together what happened and what their message was and what we were supposed to do.

The next morning, the family the angels sent us to didn't turn us away. They seemed glad for our visit. For a few months after that, we and our story enjoyed some popularity. Until Herod put an end to it. Sure, we heard the rumor that the child's family had escaped, but you know rumors. After the massacre, some blamed our story for the slaughter, so we stopped telling it. The only reason I'm telling you now is that we've heard another rumor: the child the angels sang about is a man now. The sick and blind are flocking to him. Still, we're laying low. We know better than to get our hopes up.

A CAROL   *Luke 2:20*

>   *translated from a shepherd's*
>   *original ecstatic utterance*

God is a big fish
God is an ocean
God is a tiny boat
God is from Goshen

God is from Stockholm
God is from Asia
God is from outer space
God has amnesia

God has an old house
God has a rabbit
God has an inner ear
God is no robot

God is no daydream
God is no Santa
God is no candyman
God loves Atlanta

God loves Soweto
God loves red currants
God loves to boogaloo
God comes in orange

God comes in thin crust
God comes in deep dish
God comes in swaddling cloth
God is a big fish

MIDSUMMER   *Luke 1 & 2*

Most mornings, the shhh of the neighbor's
sprinkler on a slow, automatic pass

by the holly goes unheard—the air so full
of avian chant. The new day's birth song.

But this morning, only the sprinkler
and, like white noise or tinnitus, crickets

doing their best to fill in for the birds'
polyphonous chanting now eerily absent.

Did anyone sing at my birth? When did we,
so big on requiems, stop composing birth songs?

ODE TO THE FERRYMAN   Luke 2:6

    a birth song

who, in my story,
never heard of Kharon
or Lethe, never
listened to Styx,
and calling hell *Hades*
was, I'm told, near
to cursing as he came.

To him: thank you,
belatedly, for
interceding for
me whose hurry
to see Coronado sun
triggered her labor,
their car already in line

to board your ferry
to North Island
and the naval bed
I'd be born in.
But your kind care
to load our car on first
to be first off

obviated an awkward
mid-transit delivery.
So it is right and good
to praise you

and your quick thinking,
your will to push
the ferry's engines to their max.

THE MAGI'S REPORT   Matthew 2:12

Curious Herod's reception of us
after hearing we'd received the birth announcement
from—*anathema*—the stars.
Why, had one of their own reported as much
he'd have been stoned to death.
But we've known this about them for ages—a hard people,
hardest on themselves.
That we astrologers were many
and hailed from several powerful suzerains
and bore royal gifts
all worked, no doubt, to our advantage.
But more curious still
their king sending us on to a village
miles from Jerusalem
to find the crown prince we came to honor.
We'd have turned straight home
had not the stars confirmed it. And there we found the child
in a less than modest house,
the mother herself a child, the father
a mere tradesman. All too
peculiar. Ridiculous, in fact. And then
a disturbing dream about a deceiver king
and our decision—the prince
having won our hearts—not to return to Jerusalem as requested.
On our roundabout route home,
strange news reached us:
how Herod had all the children of that village
massacred. *Children.*
May we risk impertinence?
We've no need of stars to reveal their king is horrid.

THE SWORD   Matthew 2:13–22

1.
He woke her and told her simply
to gather up the child
for they had to leave town.
"Now!"
It was still night.

2.
When a rider reached the caravan
with word of the slaughter
in Bethlehem,
the Jews among the travelers
could not be consoled.

3.
She collapsed. *It was
our boy they wanted*—the thought
a sword—old Simeon said it—
straight through her heart—their secret
compounding the ache.

4.
Bethlehem, O Bethlehem.
There will be no returning there.

ON DREAM LEARNING *Matthew 2:22*

Learned in a dream my Canadian mother
did a year at Columbia—so Barnard—where
she met Henry, whom she called Hank,
her mention of him so vivid I ran into Henry
in a West Village club where we talked—
he even taller than she led me to believe—
and when she joined us she was this guy
who, by mid-conversation, became my sister.
Which was cool, but I couldn't get from any
of them whether mother had failed out

or moved in with Henry and simply stopped
going to class. (She was too smart to fail,
so I figured the latter.) All I got was this sly
half-smile from her, now my mother again,
as she told me soon Henry would be famous,
how he'd bumped into a poet from the midwest
who thought he could pull off something big,
and I thought, here we go again, a man
her ticket out of the middle-class Canadian funk
she never was able to shake. And though

she would not have believed me, I knew then,
once his fortunes began to change, she'd
lose Henry and wind up back home in B.C.
waiting insufferably for her prince to come
and save her—which tune the house trio
played as we talked. Happily, I felt no pity
or anger, only a curious gladness for tall Henry
and joy that my mother finally opened up
about her several selves and that year in the city
she was never able to tell father about.

3

STARTING FROM NAZARETH *John 1:46*

and the unlikelihood
of anything good
to the dreamlike certainty

of great things, where
great things are topped by
even greater things,

and so on and so forth—
eye hath not seen
nor ear heard how good it gets.

THE WATCHERS

Luke 4:1–2
Mark 1:12–13

in praise of the eagle-owl, after Robert Siegel

I have brought him hyrax and nightjar,
yet he does not eat.

It baffles me, his being here
day after day—has it been a month?

When others of his kind approach
the waterhole, he withdraws

to the rocks and gullies, the shadows
by day, that small cave at night.

It makes no sense—the one who fills all
with fullness wasting away, alone.

Several of my kind have taken to watching
over him, driving off

the less comprehending predators,
our man-size wingspans terrible in their way.

And when he sleeps, we stand sentry,
our night vision good for more than just hunting.

But how long our strange duty here?
Until he dies?

Such a peculiar thought—the eternal,
who sustains all things, dying.

And what happens to us then? Would our atoms
become a startled swarm of locusts

flying off every which way?
Inconceivable. Yet here we are, he is.

And I will die protecting him, the Maker
made brother to us all.

THE MANNER OF
THEIR LEAVE TAKING   Matthew 4:18–20

I cried for weeks before the Teacher
arrived to collect my sons.
When they told us they were leaving
nets and boats for an open road,
their father, normally a quiet man,
became quieter—barely spoke at all.
So he and I waited, dreading separately
the day the Teacher would show up.

I blamed the wild-haired Baptizer
for stirring expectations
of a deliverer already among us.
But when the Teacher actually stepped
inside the door of our small house
and asked to stay for a day or so—
his manner far lovelier than his rough exterior—
we felt strangely consoled and slept well.

He had the dark face and hands of a laborer,
not at all like the pale teachers in town.
And his stories and easy laughter—
the way he spoke with us
was always comforting, familiar.
Even the morning he left with our sons,
he tried to explain so we might understand:
"They will be net casting for men."

I don't think any of us saw what he meant,
but it was alright. My quieted husband
even found his voice again,
blessed his sons, and assured them

we'd be fine. For weeks after
they walked away down the beach,
he would repeat the Teacher's words,
"net casting for men," and laugh aloud to himself.

## CAPERNAUM	*Mark 1:35*

After sunset and long into the night,
the whole town at the door.

Early next morning,
still dark, he left town

to be alone and pray.
A short sleep. Fitful perhaps.

Haunted by the ailments and faces
of those in Capernaum. And those to come.

PREPPING FOR BIBLE STUDY   *Mark 2:1*

On a quick run to Price Chopper
for the finger food, I'm still stewing
over the first verse of chapter two where,
in Greek, the verb is present tense,
the predicate simply "house." Not "home."
So Jesus in Capernaum had not, in fact,
"come home," as one translation says.
Rather "he is in the house." As in
"Elvis is in the house," the way MCs
tipped off fans pressing toward the stage
and preparing to scream. In Mark's gospel,
so many had gathered that it was SRO
in the house. And outside the gate
the crowd was even larger. And no one
wore masks or gave a thought to whether
the grocery store clerk had or had not
sanitized his conveyor belt after ringing
out the previous patron—a new delay I am
getting used to as I wait on a taped X
to be gestured to the register where
carrots, broccoli, celery, and hummus
will cross the transactional threshold
to be elevated into comestible stardom
when Paul and Judy arrive masked
for Bible study, and we sit across the room
from each other and enter into the story
to see Jesus, and watch him do his magic.

THE GENERATIVE INFLUENCE
OF Q ON JOHN'S GOSPEL Luke 5:1–11

The fragment is on the mark.
Whoever wrote it down got it right,
and I should know.

From a boat offshore,
my younger self watched it happen:
the crowd pressing upon the Teacher
as he taught on the beach;
he commandeering Peter's boat
and telling him to put out into deep water;
we rolling our eyes
when he instructed Peter to let down his net,
yet then having to help him land
that crazy haul of fish;
and finally back on the beach, the Teacher
announcing, *From now on, you will catch men.*

Ever since it was entrusted to me,
I have treasured this fragment,
holding it as first among the other fragments
I keep rolled in a scrap of leather.
And there's a new reason I hold it dear.

Early last Sabbath, the rains dampening
my eagerness for eldership here in Ephesus,
I unrolled the fragment
to refresh my sense of commissioning—
you will catch men—
when suddenly the words
turned themselves inside out
and I became dizzy, like that day

in the upper room with the Spirit-fire.
Suddenly the crowd on the beach
listening to Jesus teach the word of God
became a crowd on a beach
listening to God.
I felt myself melt, as if into a glorious light.

Then later in the day words occurred to me—
In the beginning was the Word,
and the Word was—
along with a compulsion
to write them down
and follow them with other words.
And it was as though I were once again
following Jesus up some rocky path
between small towns on the way to Jerusalem.

I'm telling this to all of you
because the idea these words convey
will be called blasphemous.
I may suffer for having written them.
But I know and trust their source,
and when I'm done they must
be sent around to all the Teacher's friends.
Which makes me nervous
how even they will receive them,
for none of the others have spoken as plainly
of the Teacher in this way—
as the great I AM. So I have awakened you,
the moon still bright above the city,
because I want you to sit with me and pray
as I write what I will write.

You know how tired I become by early afternoon,
and how I have needed your help
shepherding our little flock here in Ephesus.
Well, now I will need you even more
to help complete the new work. Please,
someone bring me my pen, ink, and parchment.

IN JOHN'S GOSPEL *John 2:3*

there is no hint of a *Bill of Rights*
or *Shorter Catechism* or *Little Red Book*.

What's there is God with us,
the Word made flesh making wine

and a whip and saying crazy shit, like
"Before Abraham was, I am," and "Come,

follow me," and "Why are you crying?
Who is it you are looking for?"

DO WHATEVER HE TELLS YOU *John 2:5*

And what if he tells you to make poems?
Not wine or disciples. Not even guitars.

WILDERNESS   *Luke 5:16*

Pocked with nests,
shallow pockets of pulse

and kind, kin and semblance,
the desert floor-

as-nursery flourishes
in its way, and he visits often,

selective always of a new path—
his presence like rain.

REPORT FROM THE FIELD   *Luke 5:17–26*

It had taken some sensitive negotiating,
but the invitation was generous:
a fully subsidized, three-day, lakeside retreat
with lodging and meals provided.
Three days with the one
some were already calling "The Teacher."
And they'd have him all to themselves, his words
and reputation as a healer
the main draw.

On the day of,
synagogue elders from every village
and town and Jerusalem too
descended on the site,
and not one spare room in Capernaum
went unfilled.
No one could remember a gathering like it,
and though the benefactor's house
was large, the number of retreatants was greater
than expected. Even important latecomers,
unable to squeeze in, stood
with recent seminary grads at open
windows and doors, straining to hear the Teacher teach
then his answers during the Q&A.

I had been assigned by a local news outlet
to cover the event—
what many were hoping would be
a rabbinic love fest of sorts,
something to help the Teacher gain traction

among the wider community of religious leaders
and expand his fan base well beyond
the sick and poor
who were known to swarm him.

But on the afternoon of the second day,
a cell of ragged interlopers,
impatient for the Teacher's attention,
removed tiles from the benefactor's roof
and lowered a cripple
not ten feet from where the Teacher sat teaching.
Needless to say, the room hushed—
half astonished at the interlopers' chutzpah,
half thrilled that they might witness a healing up close—
and the Teacher went off script.
I am not permitted to report what he said.
Suffice it to say, he blasphemed,
and the interlopers got more than what they came for.
And the once-in-a-lifetime gathering of rabbis
and other synagogue leaders
ground to a sudden halt.
And by sunset, lakeside Capernaum was quiet.

It would be an understatement to assert
the Teacher's misstep
proved disastrous to his cause.
Unless one happened to stick around after
the elite's hasty dispersal
to witness their displacement
by a steady trickle of outcasts who,
having overheard from those storming off
what the Teacher did and said,
limped nervously onto the benefactor's fabulous property
and, surrounding the large house,
waited there silently throughout the night
for the Teacher to emerge.
I close my report by noting the latter number were twice the former.

A QUICK THANK YOU   Matthew 6:7

    from God

Every morning—and it's never not morning,
so much human chatter, unlike the wantless birds

filling the air with gorgeous songs—it is nice
your stillness not adding to the verbal clutter.

Like the smoke of incense, somewhere it says
of prayer. But what did David know of being taken

for a kind of toll booth? So many passing through
depositing their two bits for road maintenance,

the expectation of smooth travel to safe destinations.
(And David knew nothing of those not of his own flock.)

So thank you for sitting here, quietly, with me.
Thank you from the well of my words-weary heart.

DO YOU WANT TO GET WELL? *John 5:6–7*

"Sir, I have no one to . . . ," but

short answer: yes.
Honest answer: yes, yet there is

that of my infirmity I love too much.
So, yes and no.

Honest, too: my wish
for singleness of heart, such

wellness as would end this coddling
of my downcast state. Still,

beyond the honest
yes and no, a final, flailing, "Yes, I do.

I want to get well, no matter what
may ensue."

BEFORE RELIGION *Luke 8:42b-44*

When only hunches tipped hearts
away from fear
and grudge and massacre

toward prudence,
contrition and praise,
holiness was not

a thing. Nor righteousness.
There was only
the heart, only hunch and wavering.

LA LA CAVEAT *Luke 9:10–17*

Much as I adore Luke,
his is the only gospel with a picnic
not followed by a boat ride.

What's that about?
Who'd want a picnic without a boat ride?
Five other times—in Matthew,

Mark, even John—a long afternoon
passes as it should: a field day
plus an excursion.

Something so right about
al fresco dining beside a lake,
then loading into a boat and shoving off.

THE EAR *Luke 9:47*

The Teacher grabbed me gently by the ear,
dragged me to the center of a circle of his friends,
had me stand beside him.

I don't remember even a little
of what he said or they talked about,
but as his leathery hand slipped from my ear

to shoulder and rested there,
I felt as welcome as I always am
at my grandmother's table or when at night

a terror drives me to my parents' bed.
When he left town, I wanted to follow but couldn't,
so for days kept a twig tucked behind the ear.

A MOVING POEM *Luke 9:60*

A new voice needs space in me.
How to clear out a self from a self?

Maybe rent a truck and dump it
somewhere, make a bonfire.

So much of what fills me must go.
Think yard sale. Bargain prices galore.

Or one big curbside giveaway,
a sign saying, *Take it; it's all free.*

SOMETIMES   John 8:12

House lights on, the sun out,
I step into darkness.

Or the dark
steps forward in me

inviting my surrender,
the way music

enlists my limbs in
movement almost dance.

Of course, were I
a dancer, mine would be

actual dance, or
if I belonged

in darkness,
surrender would be

my reflex and
I would have no want of

any light at all.
And yet

there is light,
the One—in the deepest

dark of the cosmos;
as well within the even

darker heart—who is
gentle, and winsome as light.

TO SEPARATE HEAD AND BODY   *Matthew 14:1–12*

requires,
before the brute force of it,
an act of will,
a choice, and, before that,
imagination: to see
the decapitative option
and adjudge it
desirable, an effective way
to shush the offending tongue.

Often the option is
elected by one—say, Herodias—
ordered by another—Herod—
then carried out
by the never-named executioner—
with the grisly act witnessed
by a silent throng—
say, Herod's birthday guests.
And so beheading creates community.

Actually, two communities.
The first, who nervously
applaud and release
the severed head and corpse
to the second, who
grieve, bury the dead,
and begin imagining a new world
without the first.

Enter all manner
of apocalyptic story lines
and a literature

pertaining thereto—to which
you may suppose
this poem belongs,
though you would be wrong.
For this is a love poem,
no room for plagues of frogs or blood.

Think rather grace, the whole
of humanity as one
body co-laboring under one
unsevered head who commends
each part to the other
and all to those most vulnerable.
Imagine such a better way
and John—acerbic messenger, rank
earthy angel—on loan
from mercy's sovereign throne.
Imagine the Herods choosing repentance.

CONFESSION Luke 10:20

Why do I want a fine house, fine
in style, bones, and landscaping,
with a south-facing front porch
where one day a public figure—say,
the governor—will afix a bronze plaque
to the right of the front door?

For when other poets will gather there
to observe a moment of silence,
and one of them—say, the state's
poet laureate—will read an elegy
in my honor, something I want most
after visiting other poets' homes,

especially those with classic kitchens,
open by design, with features
that intimate the writing life: *pantries*
and *freezers* to signify memory;
checkered butcher blocks and *gas stoves,*
the actual making of a thing.

If only I were not afraid to die
and amount to nothing, forgotten.
Which is why a south-facing front porch
on a fine house and a bronze plaque
visible from a well-worn sidewalk
appeals to me. And ample parking, too.

MAYBE THIS IS NOT A POEM   *Luke 12:32–33*

Hearing their cry—poverty's
wide, thick stone pressing
air from their lungs—the Teacher says

we must, after confessing self-
love, attend first to flowers
and birds—lilies, ravens, even

the common grasses of the field—
and keep attending until
it becomes clear—the kingdom—

and we see our complicity
in cutting and placing that stone
on those chests. It is another

trail of tears: from our weeping
for ourselves to weeping with
those who weep; to down-

sizing from desire to necessity;
to putting ourselves to work
lifting that suffocating stone.

Have we failed to be, as ravens
and lilies and common grass,
without rank or privilege?

Have I refused aid to the weak
and lonely, the terminally trapped
and tapped out, preferring

my comfort, pursuing my bliss?
Maybe this should not be a poem.
Or maybe this is precisely what

a poem needs to be—a cry
for all those lives disappearing
beneath that awful, suffocating stone.

PARSING   *Luke 12:49*
                                                                       John 9:5

Whether the sun's thermonuclear fire
or the match I struck this morning,

light's speed is the same, equally gentle
here, and the otherwise stubborn

dark yields to it without resistance.
Our problem is not the accommodating dark

but the difficulty sustaining any
generation of light at all. Even the stars

like these matches burn only so long,
and with darkness comes the cold.

IT WOULD BE ARSON *Luke 12:49*

what if it's true

fat with a dead old order
he bore it
till it killed him

till he was
raised changed
fat with a new fiery order

that with a wild
rush of wind he delivered
upon the world

what if it's true

he came to set
fire to the world
and make all things new

FRACTION *Luke 12:51*

One is divisible any number of ways.

Consider the cheesecake or banana or
a single night's sleep. Or he who

knew well what to do with fish and bread
and said not peace but division

must follow, all manner of griefs:
negative numbers, standard deviations,

proofs, vectors, derivatives, slope fields—
but enough of that.

Of the playing with numbers there is no end.

THE SIGN OF JONAH *Matthew 16:4*

And I don't mean the short kid
on the youth soccer team I coached
late afternoons after school,
whose over-the-top mother—despite
her embarrassed boy's seven
hat-tricks that whale of a season—
required far more coaching than he did.

Nor the shaggy sophomore Jonah
whom we called *One-Point-Oh!* whose
well-frayed and golden, wide-wale
bellbottom corduroys were so
long they seemed never to reveal
whether, that April before his May expulsion,
he ever wore shoes to class.

And even if such characters were
to abound and every one of us could tell
our own "sign of Jonah" stories,
I'm quite sure none of them would have much
if anything to teach us or be so
sign-worthy as to leave a whole house
of bishops scratching their silly-hatted heads.

Fortunately for Jesus, the day
he dropped his Jonah line on his detractors,
the saying was not yet what befuddles
new religion majors on day one
of my "Myths, Myths, & More Myths" prereq—
that first quiz a diagnostic for telling who
will likely bail, who rise and prophesy.

LA LA THANKFUL LIVING   *Matthew 19:16–22*

We so quickly tire of
those who so quickly tire of
us who so quickly tire of whatsoever

may be less than lovely.
You know who I mean, though if
you don't, we know

where you live, the mart
where you shop and where you spend
your Saturdays: namely

far from where we—
of parts far other than where you call
home—wear far lovelier

evening wear than you, consume
far lovelier cars, and carry
ourselves as we know

you so quickly tire of.
Though frankly we, lovely as
we (thankful) are, do not (boo-hoo) care.

AT TABLE

Luke 22:14
Ephesians 2:6

Infinitesimal and of no consequence
but for the daft valuation of divine Love—

by whom a body is made no larger,
no more visible from the ridge opposite,

yet through whom a body is seated
in the heavenlies, where—this, a mystery—

it offers no service at that high table.
And so a body here is free of setting for itself

a place at any earthly table, free indeed
to stand aside and, in the grace of

such a love, wait on all reclined around it.
Which is, of course, absurd—the very

idea of transcending value—even desperate.
To the praise of God: a body, nonsensical.

AND WHEN IT IS DRY? *Luke 23:31*

The tree is green,
the fairways immaculate,
the caviar divine.

Who can blame you-
know-who for building a wall?

RUNNING TO WIN   *Matthew 22:31–32*

Rounding the far turn into autumn
it's anybody's race, the field

never more crowded, not even the dead
are dead to him who, at once, waits

at the finish and runs among us
and leads the pack into this year's

home stretch, our ears trained, at once,
on his voice and the hallooing

of angels all along the way—forever
the same prize, never the same

magnificent circuit. *How many laps to go?*
on every last plodder's mind but his.

UNATTENDED *Luke 23:43*

Rain or shine, the neighbor's lawn sprinkler begins
a percussive song and dance before sunrise.
I am learning to leave off with things that require
my curation and settle in with all that thrives
unattended: the spin and course of earth and moon,

the wind and clouds, fullness of the seasons, cycles
of plant and animal flourishing and extinction.
I cannot say yet that I'm fine with the thought of my
dying, though I know it happens to the best of us,
attended or unattended, no escaping the inevitable.

And that will be that, finis. Or maybe it will be as
the neighbor's automated lawn sprinkler, so
when we've given all we've got to give, we sleep—
what looks to us more like a return to oblivion
but is our good energy resting for the next new day.

And yet this hope too requires curation, the work
of belief and holding fast and making revisions
or refusing revisions that may obviate the myth
as originally conceived. Is it faithless to leave off
with our small cartoons of what will happen when

or next or not at all? Or is it rather the gist of faith,
this uncertainty of either elsewhere or nowhere?
Can I live and die content beneath the broad shadow
of such a large irresolution? What are my options
really? Anxiety, it seems to me, or trust. And only these.

IN MORNING SUNLIGHT   *Mark 10:13–16*

Squam Lake, NH

It was beautiful and black
against the mottling browns
on the lake bottom off the dock

and swam in slowly as if
to fool a prey into thinking
it had recently feasted.

On the dock, barefooted, maybe
ten, I pulled here and there
on the line tangled in my reel,

pulse racing, cursing my luck
and whoever left it that way.
Likely a younger brother.

As the huge bass drew near
the dock's end and deep shadow
underneath, I could see

the broad gills calmly troubling
the cold water for oxygen,
my breaths coming in gasps

or maybe I didn't breathe at all
as I worked the tangle furiously.
This would not be the last time

a big and beautiful fish
would slip even the possibility
of my grasp, but it was the first.

And when it slowly turned
a casual pivot back out toward
the lake's shifting mystery

and depth, I slowly sat down
on that sturdy dock's slatted edge
in tears, watching it disappear.

CREDO   John 11:23–26
                                                  Luke 24:11

for my father

He is disappearing from himself.
She is learning to spend time

away from him, out with new friends
for dinner, a show, a nightcap.

He does not know that he was left
with a nurse to feed him his lasagna.

He does not recognize the fork.
And on the far side of

a wall he hasn't a clue is there,
his whole life waits to be returned

to him—in the resurrection, a bit
of nonsense I believe because the idea

is beautiful: *What is sown mortal
will be raised immortal.*

HOW IT WILL BE *John 11:23–26*
Revelation 21:5

Each old thing a door
for the new thing pressing
on the old from within,

not to erase the old thing
but to step forward in
and through the old,

the way every cell of his
body all at once yielded to
the power pressing from

within, and he was made
new, never more alive, first-
born from the dead. And

that's how it will be: each
old thing a door the new
will step clear through

into new light, new air—
all doors, all bodies,
nothing not made new.

WHAT DIFFERENCE DOES IT MAKE   *John 15:12*

factoring for Welsh or Slavic or Dane,
Tiot or Carib or Ghanan?

Besides the historical, which is not
nothing, we face the categorical

day to day of loving one another,
not only our own kith, and blessing

the good ground beneath our feet.
We've only, to begin, to listen

till we see in the face of the other
the beautiful other we are to love.

But I'm preaching again, as though
I've got this, which my heart tells me

I haven't. Though who has? Aren't we,
whether Welsh or Tiot or Ghanan,

mired here, inept at love yet longing
for those rains to water the earth

between us and bring forth trees
with leaves for healing the nations

and, month to month, fruit to feed us all?
We can dream, can't we? No, we must.

THEY WILL RESPECT MY SON   *Matthew 21:37*

who did small things well:
bless children, throw together
meals for his friends,
speak quietly of a kingdom come.

Who wanted only for the good
of all—even of the few
who wanted him to disappear,
wishing he would die. You'd think

they would speak well of him.
You'd think perhaps be grateful
he did not delete them
and their story, then and there.

You'd think, at least,
they would respect him for his many
kindnesses toward the sad
and undeserving likes of us.

WHEN THE END COMES

Matthew 24
Revelation 11:18

and those who destroy the earth
are destroyed,
will I be among them
for my complicity in their schemes—
watching from outside
as every last other thing undergoes
molecular transformation—
as happened to the body
of the Word—and each good begun is,
as imagined at its beginning,
carried forward to glorious consummation?

When it comes,
will I marvel when all cars
and highways dematerialize, all
drivers and passengers
fly into clear sky, the elect knowing
without a moment of panic
how to air-swim
as they set out unencumbered
for the shore or mountains or throne of grace,
each arriving in a blink
or after a leisurely tour?

I am not a fan
of those versions of the apocalypse
that terrify me—that seem
rooted in rage or revenge.
True, what has been badly blighted
must be removed
and the means may be painful indeed,

but how I wish to slip the fate
of earth's destroyers and awaken
mid-flight, high above some former byway,
clear-eyed and still breathing.

DO NOT THINK THIS IS   *Matthew 25:31–46*

with a line attributed somewhere to Langston Hughes

Do not think this is
about language
or ambition, fashion
or some overflow of feeling.
There is far more
at stake here than these.

The poor toil
among us; prisoners
languish elsewhere; the sick
and impaired await
aid; the oppressed cry out
for release.

Lilies are under threat
and sequoias,
the birds of the air,
all things
that live on land
and swim in earth's waters.

This is about beauty
and goodness; whatever
is true and noble,
right, pure, and admirable—
no matter how offensive
the saying of it

or hard to live it out.
The target's mark remains

the target's mark:
write the love poem
for the planet
and our being, together, here.

WHEN THE SUN STOPPED SHINING   *Luke 23:44–46*

Brother Sun closed his eye,
a humble act of deference.
Or was it that he could not watch
    his maker die?

For Joshua, the sun stood still;
in Kings, reversed direction.
Or was it just to make a point
    as stories will?

I'd rather not an argument
(as though to win were all),
but skate the seas on blades of light
    and never fall.

4

TRESPASSING
ON THE MOUNT OF OLIVES   Luke 22:39, 47

> *MOUNT OLIVE – A 19-year-old was arrested on trespassing charges over the weekend when he entered a house without permission and fell asleep on the couch . . . . He was released on his own recognizance and has a pending court appearance.*
>
>   *– from The Star Ledger, found on NJ.com*

The young man claimed he thought it was a friend's house,
inebriation—no surprise—having scrambled his familiar world.

There was no malice intended, no evidence of a forced entry,
no resistance in the morning when the homeowner arranged

for an officer to escort the lad courteously to a squad car.
Though I have never awakened on a strange couch

in a stranger's house, I did wake up into sentience in the early
Sixties thinking, *Where am I?* and *What am I doing here?*

Though I have never been to Mount Olive, New Jersey,
I have spent years of my reading life on the Mount of Olives,

trespassing, looking for a brown-skinned teacher I never met
growing up in white, post-war, Episcopalian America.

A rough, street-level itinerant, he recalibrated the good life,
lavishing crazy affection on outcasts, the immoral, and others

like me, and pitched his camp in that grove where it's rumored
he sweat blood and suffered betrayal and, when swords

were drawn to defend him, parried sharply, "Enough of that!"
This morning in Connecticut, I've again ascended the Mount

wondering, *Where is he?* and *What on earth am I doing here?*—
wanting more than anything to stay alive a little longer,

long enough to see our son joyful, our marriage more than
you or I could have imagined; my own court appearance pending.

Notes

"Hymn"
The quotation in the opening stanza is Anselm's ontological argument, from his *Proslogion*.

"Man with Water Jar"
The painting referred to in section one is imagined.

"The Women"
Women in early Jewish society were organized apart from the men, and tradition kept them apart. This poem and others in *Trespassing* imagines Jesus using this cultural arrangement counter-culturally to accomplish his mission.

"Ἐν ἀρχῇ"
Greek: "In the beginning"

"Venit"
Latin: "He came"

"What Matters Moves"
Janeway of *Star Trek: Voyager* fame

"A Carol"
The original ecstatic utterance is, of course, imagined.

"Generative Influence of Q"
Events recorded in the gospels are thought by scholars to have earlier (lost) written sources. "Q" is one of them. Here I imagine St. John as having acquired a fragment of the Q source.

Notes

"Do You Want to Get Well?"
The phrase "my downcast state" echos the phrase in Shakespeare's Sonnet 29 – "my outcast state" – a poem that saved my life after I was laid off in 2009.

"Sometimes"
NASA has found in deep space "visible light that's not connected to any known source." Greenfieldboyce, Nell. "Scientists Discover Outer Space Isn't Pitch-Black After All." https://www.npr.org/2020/11/18/936219170/scientists-discover-outer-space-isnt-pitch-black-after-all.

"Credo"
The closing lines lean on (1) the apostles' initial judgment on the resurrection report of the women in Luke 24—that it was *leiros* (nonsense, poppycock)—and (2) the Keats aphorism from "Ode on a Grecian Urn," *Beauty is truth, truth beauty.* So my calling the nonsense a beautiful idea is simply another way of affirming my love for the truth of the women's report and the resurrection. Thus, the confidence in the quotation from Saint Paul in 1 Corinthians 15.

"When the End Comes"
The poem begins with a troubling question: Is it possible for a believer to be so on board with the systems that are destroying the earth that s/he suffers the fate of the destroyers? After all, a believer, who is not on the side of the earth and the poor, misses the point that Jesus was anointed to "proclaim the year of the Lord's favor" (Luke 4:18-19) which includes practical loving care for the earth and its creatures. A fully biblical faith summons believers to aim at loving what and who God loves and believing in and with Jesus. Such faith embraces practical, loving care for the earth and opposes its destruction. Thus, the question of the first stanza.

Also, there are eschatologies that assume the end of history will occur at some point in the future when God breaks into time and space (from outside) to take control and dispense with judgment on the wicked world. These eschatologies begin with the good assumption that God is transcendent and so, for now, from elsewhere. The eschatology in my poem (and others in Trespassing) is different. It begins with thinking of God as immanent – Immanuel – the one who presently rules "over, through, and in all things" (Ephesians 4:6) and

Notes

by whose power all things are held in being, sustained moment to moment through time. Even those things that currently break God's heart. This immanental eschatology assumes that "the end" and the judgment began in history with the resurrection of Jesus and is continuing to arrive, "on earth as it is in heaven," as God steps forward (ever so slowly, it seems) from within creation to eventually and suddenly transform, as though in one fell swoop, the whole kit and caboodle. Transcendence is not obviated; God rules over all things. But God is also immanent, ruling through and in all things. It's a both/and proposition. So as Jesus' body was changed within time and space, so too all things will be changed. The poem presents a cartoon of the day when this from-the-inside-out transformation is finally and fell-swoopishly completed.

Acknowledgments

So much of any collection is a collaboration between writer and friends, writer and (if/then) spouse, writer and editors. In this regard, I am indebted chiefly to Bob Cording, Deb Davis, and Don Martin for their supportive, critical responses to drafts of these poems. And of course to those who read them and managed a few kind words to endorse the book, thank you.

I am also deeply grateful for the editors who saw fit to publish the following poems (or earlier versions) in print and/or online:

Connecticut River Review: In Morning Light, Do Not Think This Is
Ekstasis: The Generative Influence of Q on John's Gospel, Report from the Field
Image: What Matters Moves
JAMA: Credo
LETTERS: Annunciation, A Mother's Work
Poems for Ephesians: At Table
Practical Theology: Hymn, Parsing, Wilderness
Presence: A Carol
Rock & Sling: Judas of the Suburbs
Solum Literary Journal: Man with Water Jar, That Sabbath, Bread & Fish, The Manner of Their Leave Taking, Before Religion

"Man with Water Jar" was a finalist for the 2020 Tom Howard Poetry Prize, and "Romsey *Christus*" appeared in the pop-up online exhibit IN/BREAK, sponsored by Transept, a group associated with the Institute for Theology, Imagination and the Arts at the University of St. Andrews, Scotland.

Finally, a huge thank you to Barry Moser, my art teacher at Williston Academy, for the use of his masterful print. And to Lindsay Lehman, former colleague from Pomfret School, for the digital image of the Moser print.

The Poiema Poetry Series

COLLECTIONS IN THIS SERIES INCLUDE:

Six Sundays toward a Seventh by Sydney Lea
Epitaphs for the Journey by Paul Mariani
Within This Tree of Bones by Robert Siegel
Particular Scandals by Julie L. Moore
Gold by Barbara Crooker
A Word In My Mouth by Robert Cording
Say This Prayer into the Past by Paul Willis
Scape by Luci Shaw
Conspiracy of Light by D.S. Martin
Second Sky by Tania Runyan
Remembering Jesus by John Leax
What Cannot Be Fixed by Jill Pelaez Baumgaertner
Still Working It Out by Brad Davis
The Hatching of the Heart by Margo Swiss
Collage of Seoul by Jae Newman
Twisted Shapes of Light by William Jolliff
These Intricacies by David Harrity
Where the Sky Opens by Laurie Klein
True, False, None of the Above by Marjorie Maddox
The Turning Aside anthology edited by D.S. Martin
Falter by Marjorie Stelmach
Phases by Mischa Willett
Second Bloom by Anya Krugovoy Silver
Adam, Eve, & the Riders of the Apocalypse anthology edited by D.S. Martin
Your Twenty-First Century Prayer Life by Nathaniel Lee Hansen
Habitation of Wonder by Abigail Carroll
Ampersand by D.S. Martin
Full Worm Moon by Julie L. Moore
Ash & Embers by James A. Zoller
The Book of Kells by Barbara Crooker
Reaching Forever by Philip C. Kolin
The Book of Bearings by Diane Glancy
In a Strange Land anthology edited by D.S. Martin
What I Have I Offer With Two Hands by Jacob Stratman
Slender Warble by Susan Cowger
Madonna, Complex by Jen Stewart Fueston
No Reason by Jack Stewart
Abundance by Andrew Lansdown
Angelicus by D.S. Martin

www.ingramcontent.com/pod-product-compliance
Lightning Source LLC
LaVergne TN
LVHW041301080426
835510LV00009B/823